READY FOR A RESCUE!

Make Your Own
PAW Patrol VEHICLES

READY FOR A RESCUE! Make Your Own PAW Patrol Vehicles
ISBN: 978-1-948206-49-5

Curiosity Books is a registered trademark of Curiosity Ink Media, LLC
www.curiosityinkmedia.com
Printed in Korea

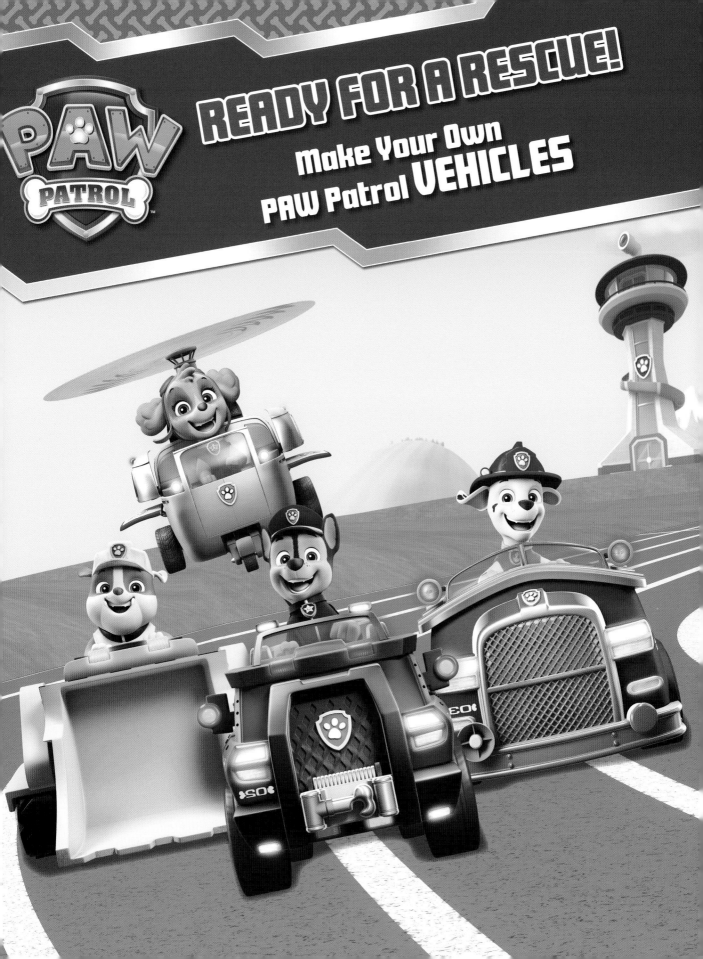

READY FOR A RESCUE!

Calling all crafty kids! Are you ruff ruff ready for an artistic adventure? The PAW Patrol is here to help you create pup-tacular vehicles! Just follow the step-by-step instructions in this book to make your very own rescue vehicles. PAW Patrol is on a roll!

WHEN MAKING AND CREATING, IT'S IMPORTANT TO ALWAYS TAKE CARE!

- Ask an adult to help when using scissors.

- Cover surfaces and open the window when using glue and paint.

- Get permission to use any materials.

TABLE OF CONTENTS

LET'S GO, PAW PATROL!

The PAW Patrol always has the right vehicles ready to race to the rescue around Adventure Bay and save the day. Find out which PAWsome tools and gadgets each vehicle has on board to get the job done!

MARSHALL'S TRUCK HAS . . .

- a ladder to reach up high
- a hose to spray water
- a flashing light for emergencies

CHASE'S POLICE TRUCK HAS . . .

- cones to block the road
- a winch to grab and pull
- a megaphone to give directions

PAW PATROL, READY FOR ACTION!

RUBBLE'S DIGGER HAS . . .

- a scoop to shovel dirt and rocks
- a drill to make holes
- wide tracks to keep from sinking in mud

ROCKY'S RECYCLING TRUCK HAS . . .

- arms to lift heavy objects
- sturdy wheels to keep level
- a large container to store objects to reuse

PUPS AWAY!

SKYE'S HELICOPTER HAS . . .

- a hook to grab and lift people, animals, and items
- cables to carry objects
- rotor blades to fly

ZUMA'S HOVERCRAFT HAS . . .

- an air cushion hull to travel over water, land, mud, and ice
- air blowers to move the craft
- an arm to reach and rescue

Vehicles make lots of pup-tastic noises. Say the words below to sound just like the vehicles in Adventure Bay!

Toot toot!	Whoosh!
Beep beep!	Screech!
Chug chug!	Honk!
Vroom!	

PAW PATROL – LET'S ROLL!

RUFF RUFF FIRE TRUCK!

Marshall is all fired up and ready to save the day! Whenever there's an emergency, his truck will be there in a flash.

Follow these steps to make a big, red fire truck just like Marshall's!

WHAT YOU NEED

- empty half gallon milk carton
- paintbrush
- red, black, and gray paint
- straws

- cardboard
- pencil
- black marker
- safety scissors
- glue
- craft sticks

WHAT TO DO

1 Make sure your milk carton is clean and dry, then fold down the open end and glue it to make a closed rectangular box. Let dry.

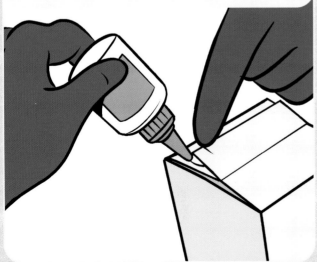

2 Paint the box red. Let dry.

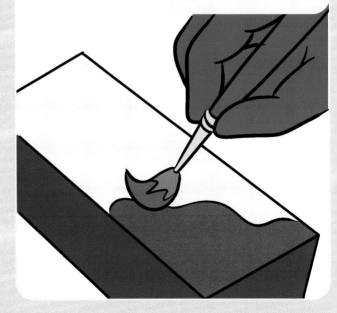

3

Carefully push a pencil through the box, twice on each side, where the wheels will be.

4

Slot a straw through the front two holes in the box, and another straw through the back two holes.

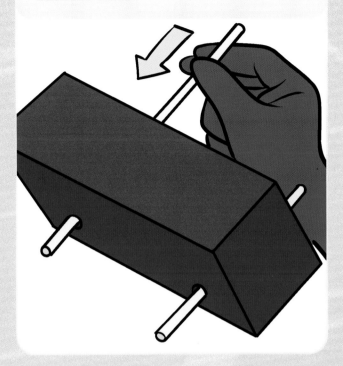

5

Ask an adult to help you cut out four circles from cardboard, to be the wheels. Paint the cardboard circles black. Let dry.

6

Carefully push a pencil through the center of each cardboard circle.

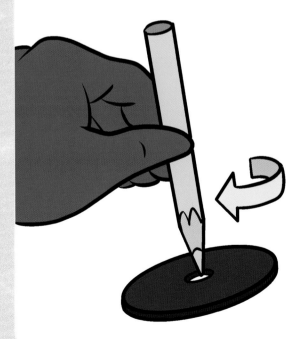

7

Slot a cardboard circle onto both ends of each straw. Trim the straw, leaving a little bit sticking out from the cardboard circles to stop them from falling off.

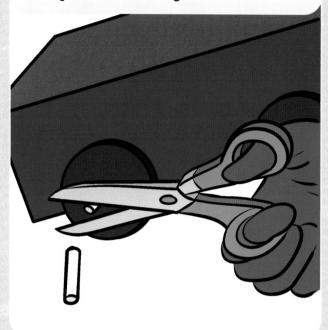

8

Ask an adult to help you cut or snap three craft sticks in half.

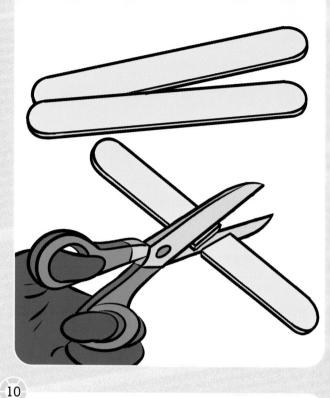

9

Set two other craft sticks parallel to each other and then place the half craft sticks across them, with a gap between each, to create a ladder. Glue the ends of the half craft sticks in place. Let dry.

10

Paint the craft stick ladder gray. Let dry.

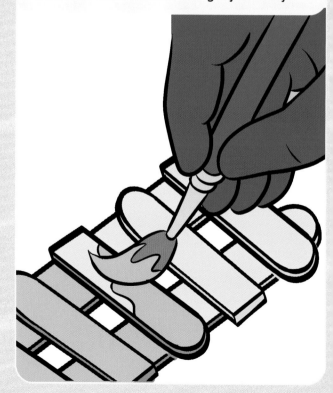

11 Glue the craft stick ladder along the top of the box. Let dry.

12 Pop out the fire truck details from the back of the book and glue them onto the box. Let dry. Add any extra details with black marker.

MARSHALL'S FIRE TRUCK IS READY TO RESCUE!

PUP-TASTIC POLICE TRUCK

Whenever anyone in Adventure Bay needs help, Chase is on the case!
His police truck is always ready to roll and race to the rescue.

Here's how you can create a truck just like everyone's favorite police pup!

WHAT YOU NEED

- 1 half-dozen egg carton
- paintbrush
- blue and black paint
- straws
- cardboard
- pencil
- black marker
- safety scissors
- glue
- orange cardstock

WHAT TO DO

1 Make sure your egg carton is clean and dry, then fold down the top and glue it to make a closed box. The bumps will be the top. Let dry.

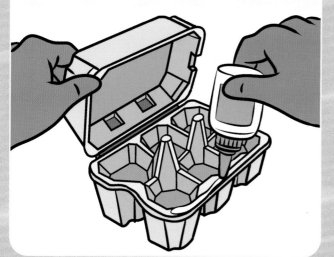

2 Paint the box blue. Let dry.

3

Carefully push a pencil through the box, twice on each side, where the wheels will be.

4

Slot a straw through the front two holes in the box, and another straw through the back two holes.

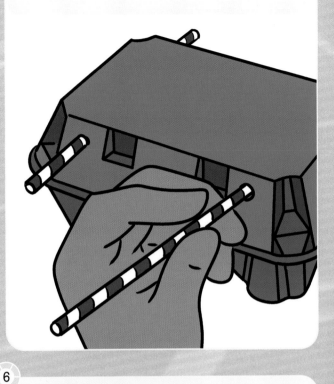

5

Ask an adult to help you cut out four circles from cardboard, to be the wheels. Paint the cardboard circles black. Let dry.

6

Carefully push a pencil through the center of each cardboard circle.

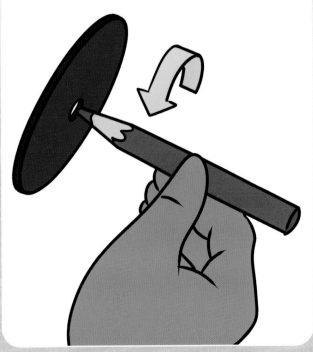

7 Slot a cardboard circle onto both ends of each straw. Trim the straw, leaving a little bit sticking out from the cardboard circles to stop them from falling off.

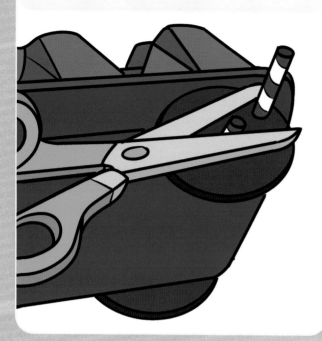

8 Cut two circles of orange cardstock, then cut each of them in half.

9 Roll each circle into a cone-shape and glue. Let dry.

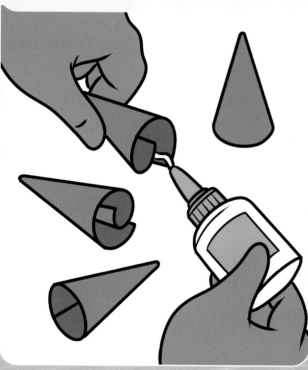

10 Glue each cone onto one of the tops of the egg-carton bumps. Let dry.

11 Pop out the police truck details from the back of the book and glue them onto the egg carton. Let dry.

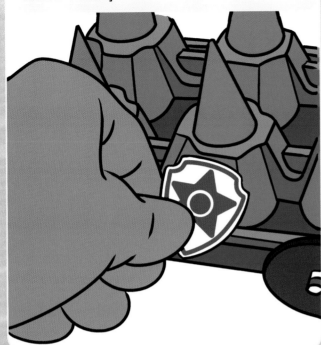

12 Add any extra details with black marker.

CHASE'S POLICE TRUCK PROTECTS ADVENTURE BAY!

ON THE DOUBLE DIGGER

This construction pup is always ruff ruff ready to dig, shovel, and shift. His digger is built to last!

Want a digger of your own? Then follow these steps to build one!

WHAT YOU NEED

- empty cereal box
- paintbrush
- yellow and gray paint
- 3 cardboard tubes
- straw
- black cardstock
- black marker
- safety scissors
- glue

WHAT TO DO

1 Fold down the open end of the cereal box and glue it closed. Let dry.

2 Paint the box yellow. Let dry.

3 Glue two cardboard tubes together along their length. Let dry.

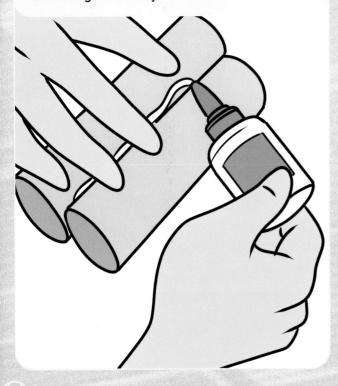

4 Cut two long strips of black cardstock—long enough to wrap around the two joined cardboard tubes.

5 Wrap one long strip of black cardstock all the way around the two joined cardboard tubes. Glue in place. Let dry.

6 Glue the cereal box on top of the two joined cardboard tubes, which form the wheel tracks on either side.

7

Cut another cardboard tube in half lengthwise, to form a scoop. Paint yellow. Let dry.

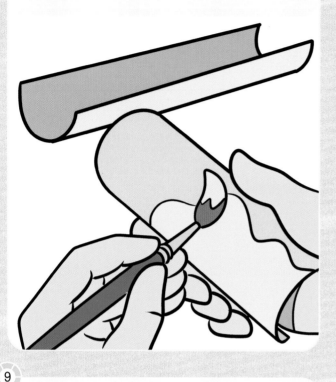

8

Glue the cardboard tube scoop onto the front of the cereal box, with the wheel tracks on either side.

9

Paint a straw gray. Let dry. With black marker, add a spiral detail looping down and around the straw to make a drill.

RUBBLE'S READY TO DIG, DIG, DIG!

Cut the straw drill to size and glue it onto the back of the cereal box. Let dry.

Pop out the digger details from the back of the book and glue them onto the box. Let dry. Add any extra details with black marker.

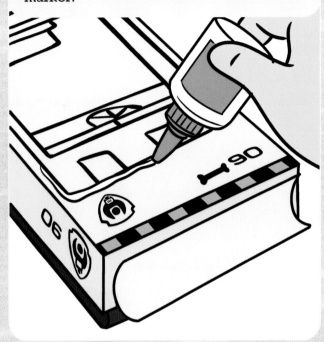

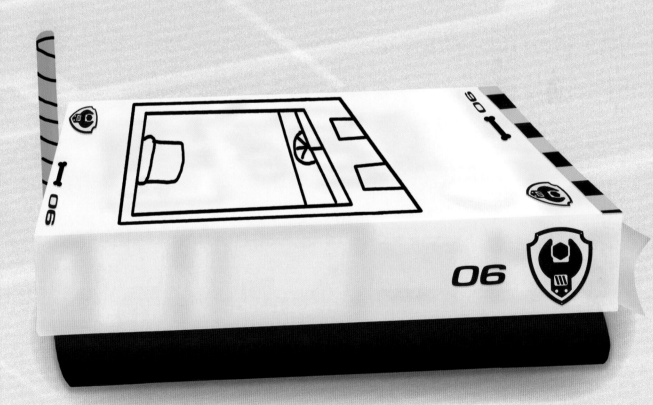

PUP PUP RECYCLING TRUCK

Rocky is one creative canine! Inside his recycling truck, he keeps all the objects he finds around Adventure Bay. Then whenever something is broken, he has just the right part to make the repair.

From a wind turbine to a playground swing, Rocky can fix anything!

WHAT YOU NEED

- empty milk carton
- paintbrush
- green, black, and orange paint
- straws
- cardboard
- pencil
- black marker
- safety scissors
- glue

WHAT TO DO

1

Make sure your milk carton is clean and dry, then cut right along the top of the open end. This will be the back of the truck.

Cut down either side of the open end to create two flaps that open, top and bottom. Paint the carton green. Let dry.

Carefully push a pencil through the carton, twice on each side, where the wheels will be. Slot a straw through the front two holes in the carton, and another straw through the back two holes.

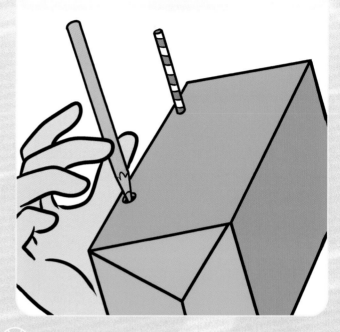

Ask an adult to help you cut out four circles from cardboard, to be the wheels. Carefully push a pencil through the center of each cardboard circle. Paint the cardboard circles black. Let dry.

Slot a cardboard circle onto both ends of each straw. Trim the straw, leaving a little bit sticking out from the cardboard circles to stop them from falling off.

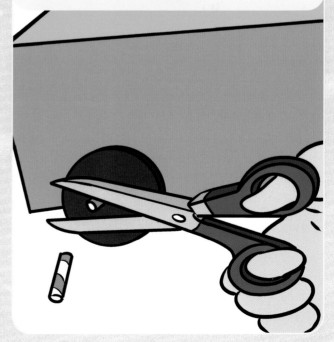

Paint two straws orange. Let dry. Then bend each of the straws in two places and glue one on either side of the carton, over the front wheels.

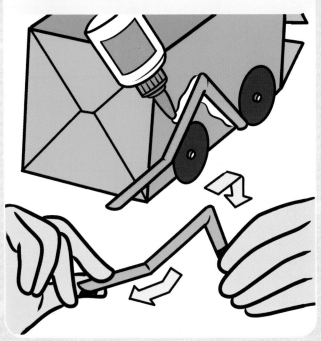

Pop out the recycling truck details from the back of the book and glue them onto the carton. Let dry. Add any extra details with black marker.

WHY TRASH IT WHEN YOU CAN STASH IT?

THE HELPFUL HERO'S HOVERCRAFT

Whether someone needs help on land or sea, Zuma zooms to the rescue with his super-speedy hovercraft. This water-loving Labrador is always ready for the next high seas adventure. Here's how to make a hovercraft just like Zuma's. Surf's pup!

WHAT YOU NEED

- black balloon
- empty, rectangular butter or margarine spread tub
- paintbrush
- orange and blue paint
- PVA glue
- 2 small, empty yogurt containers (4-5 oz)
- black marker
- safety scissors
- regular glue

WHAT TO DO

1
Remove the lid and make sure your margarine spread tub base is clean and dry.

2
Mix 50% orange paint with 50% PVA glue.

3

Paint the margarine spread tub base orange, using the paint and PVA glue mix. Let dry.

4

Blow up a black balloon just enough until it fits snugly inside the margarine spread tub base—it should still be a bit floppy. Glue it in place with regular glue. Let dry.

5

Make sure your two small yogurt containers are clean and dry. Ask an adult to help you cut the base off of both, about an inch.

6

Paint the outside of the yogurt container bases orange, using the paint and PVA glue mix. Let dry.

7

Paint a blue circle in the center of each yogurt container base, using a 50/50 mix of paint and PVA glue. Let dry.

8

Glue a small section of each yogurt container base to the back of the margarine spread tub, one sticking out on either side. Let dry.

9

Pop out the hovercraft details from the back of the book and glue them onto the tub. Let dry.

10

Add any extra details with black marker.

READY, SET, GET WET!

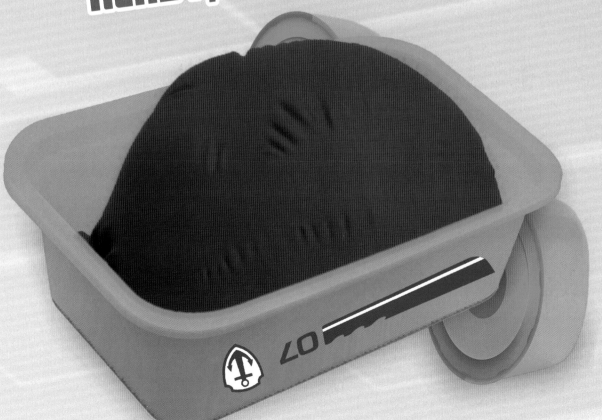

HIGH FLYING HELICOPTER

Skye might be mini . . . but she's mighty! This PAWfect pilot can see all over Adventure Bay, whether she's in her copter or she's soaring with the wings in her PupPack. These steps will help you create your own helicopter, just like Skye's. Pups away!

WHAT YOU NEED

- 2 half-dozen egg cartons
- paintbrush
- black, pink, and gray or silver paint
- straws
- cardboard
- pencil
- black marker
- safety scissors
- glue
- pipe cleaners

WHAT TO DO

1 Make sure your two egg cartons are clean and dry, then cut the top half—without the bumps—off both and glue them together to form a closed box. Let dry.

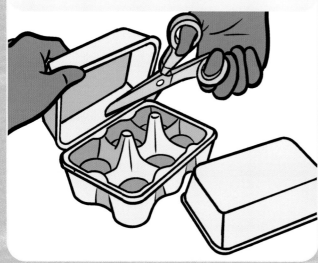

2 Paint the box gray—or silver if you have it! Let dry.

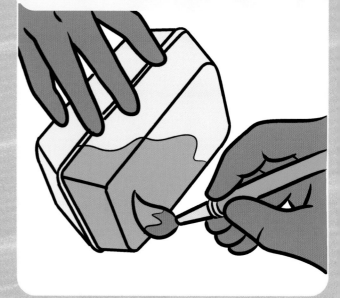

3 Ask an adult to help you cut out three circles from cardboard, two the same size and one slightly smaller, to be the wheels. Paint the cardboard circles black. Let dry.

4 Carefully push a pencil through the center of the two same-size cardboard circles.

5 Carefully push a pencil through the box, once on each side toward the back, where the wheels will be.

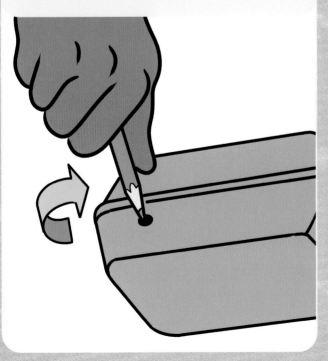

6 Slot a straw through the two side holes in the box.

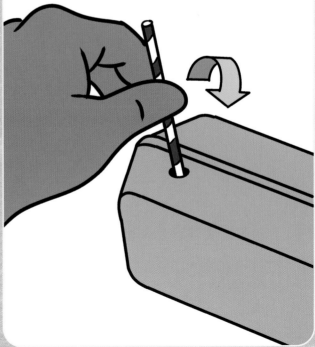

7

Slot one of the same-size cardboard circles onto each end of the straw. Trim the straw, leaving a little bit sticking out from the cardboard circles to stop them from falling off.

8

Ask an adult to help you cut a small slit at the bottom of the front of the box. Slot the smaller cardboard circle into the slot and glue in place. Let dry.

9

Carefully push a pencil through the top of the box, toward the back. Then paint a straw pink. Let dry.

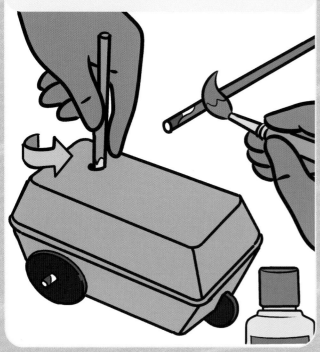

10

Push the tips of several pipe cleaners into one end of the straw. Glue them in place. Let dry. Then bend the pipe cleaners so they all splay out, like helicopter blades.

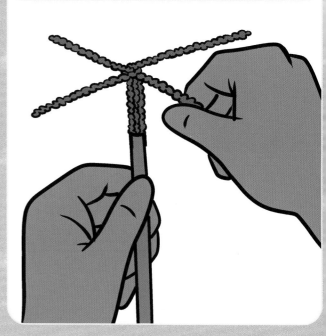

11 Slot the bottom of the straw through the hole in the top of the box.

12 Pop out the helicopter details from the back of the book and glue them onto the box. Let dry. Then add any extra details with black marker.

READY FOR TAKE OFF!

SNOW COOL SNOWCAT

Whoosh! Everest's speedy snowcat helps her race to the rescue whenever someone gets stuck on Jake's Mountain.

Follow these steps to make a snowcat as cool as Everest's!

WHAT YOU NEED

- 2 half-dozen egg cartons
- gray, white, and turquoise paint
- black cardstock
- straws
- pencil
- black marker
- safety scissors
- glue
- tape
- paintbrush

WHAT TO DO

1

Make sure your two egg cartons are clean and dry, then cut off the top half—the part without the bumps—on both cartons and glue them together to form a closed box. Let dry.

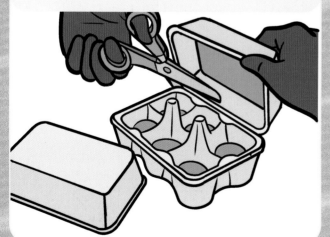

2

Paint the bottom half of the box gray and the top half white. Let dry.

3 Roll two tubes from black cardstock, one larger than the other. Add a strip of tape to secure the roll.

4 Ask an adult to help you cut holes in the box, two on each side. One larger hole should be toward the front to fit the larger card tube, and a smaller hole toward the back to fit the smaller card tube.

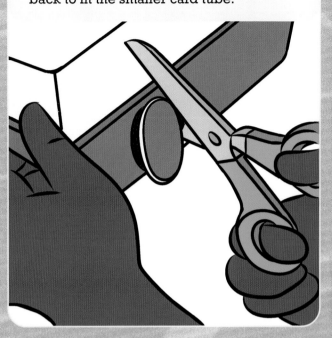

5 Slot the thicker card tube through the front two holes in the box, and the thinner card tube through the back two holes.

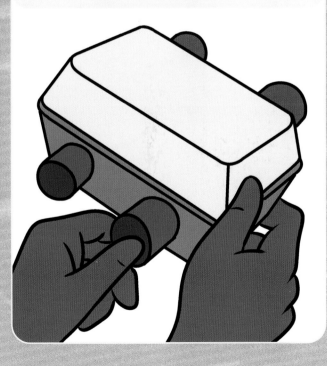

6 Cut two long strips of black cardstock—long enough to wrap around the two card tubes.

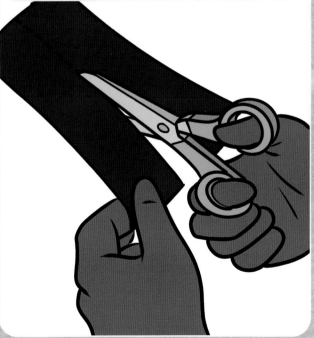

7

Wrap one strip of black cardstock around the large and small cardstock tubes on one side of the box and the other strip around the other side. Glue in place. Let dry.

8

Glue two straws into a T shape. Let dry. Then trim the top straw of the T so that it is about an inch long. Paint the straws turquoise. Let dry.

9

Carefully push a pencil through the top of the box, toward the back. Slot the long straw of the T through the hole in the top of the box.

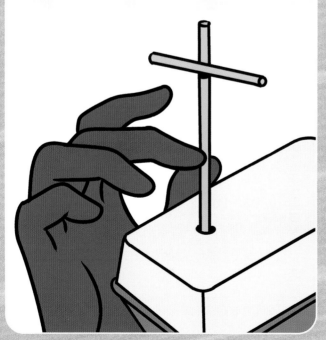

10

Pop out the snowcat details from the back of the book and glue them onto the box. Let dry. Add any extra details with black marker.

HIT THE SLOPES!

BORN TO BE WILD JUNGLE CRUISER

In his green jungle patroller, nothing can stop Tracker! His vehicle is perfect for going over rocky terrain and through swinging vines!

There's no rescue too wild for this tough pup. Here's how to create a jungle cruiser of your own.

WHAT YOU NEED

- empty cereal box
- paintbrush
- white, green, and black paint
- pencil
- safety scissors
- glue
- straws
- cardboard
- black marker

WHAT TO DO

1

Fold down the open end of the cereal box and glue it closed. Let dry. Then paint the box white with green stripes. Let dry.

2

Carefully push a pencil through the box, twice on each side, where the wheels will be. Slot a straw through the front two holes in the box, and another straw through the back two holes.

3

Ask an adult to help you cut out four circles from cardboard, to be the wheels. Paint the cardboard circles black. Let dry. Carefully push a pencil through the center of each cardboard circle.

4

Slot a cardboard circle onto both ends of each straw. Trim the straw, leaving a little bit sticking out from the cardboard circles to stop them from falling off.

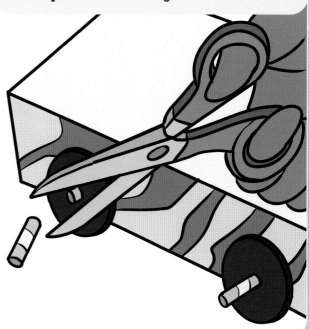

5

Paint a straw green. Let dry. Then bend the straw twice, so it has three sections. Flatten the two end sections.

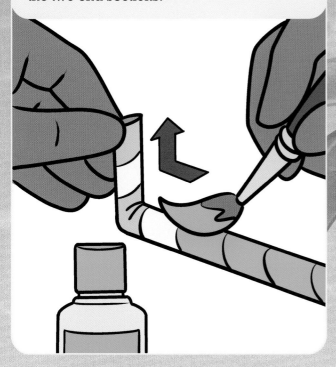

¡AL RESCATE, AMIGOS!

Glue the flat ends of the straw on either side of the box, at the back. Let dry. Pop out the jeep details from the back of the book and glue them onto the box. Let dry. Add extra details with black marker.

IT'S A JUNGLE OUT THERE!

ACTION PACKED ATV

ATV stands for "all terrain vehicle" and it's the perfect thing for a hero who performs rescues everywhere! Sand, pavement, rocks, grass, snow . . . there's nothing this quad can't handle. Get ready to roll with the pack by building your own ATV!

WHAT YOU NEED

- small, plastic empty drink bottle
- red, blue, and black paint
- PVA glue
- 3 straws
- cardboard
- pencil
- blue cardstock
- black marker
- safety scissors
- glue
- paintbrush

WHAT TO DO

1

Make sure your plastic bottle is clean and dry. Mix 50% red paint with 50% PVA glue. Paint the bottle red. Then mix 50% blue paint with 50% PVA glue and paint the bottle cap blue. Let dry.

2 Lay the bottle down on its side. Ask an adult to help you cut small holes in the bottle, twice on each side, where the wheels will be.

3 Slot a straw through the front two holes in the bottle, toward the cap, and another straw through the back two holes.

4 Ask an adult to help you cut out four circles from cardboard, two slightly larger and two slightly smaller, to be the wheels. Paint the cardboard circles black. Let dry. Carefully push a pencil through the center of each cardboard circle.

5 Slot a cardboard circle onto both ends of each straw, the larger circles toward the back of the bottle and the smaller circles toward the front. Trim the straw, leaving a little bit sticking out from the cardboard circles to stop them from falling off.

6

Paint a straw black. Let dry. Then glue the straw horizontally across the top of the bottle, above the front wheels. Let dry. Trim the straw, so it doesn't stick out any farther than the front wheels.

7

Cut two strips of blue colored cardstock. Bend each cardstock strip into a V shape and glue one on either side of the bottle, curving over the wheels. Let dry.

8

Pop out the ATV details from the back of the book and glue them onto the box. Let dry. Add any extra details with black marker.

IT'S TEAMWORK TIME!

THE PAW PATROLLER

When it's all paws on deck, the pups jump on board the PAW Patroller. There's room for everyone AND all their vehicles. They can even watch their favorite TV show *Apollo the Super-Pup* or play Pup Pup Boogie inside! By following these steps, you can create your own big bus, just like the PAW Patroller.

WHAT YOU NEED

- 1-pint empty milk carton
- 1-quart, empty milk carton
- pipe cleaners
- paintbrush
- black, red, and gray or silver paint
- straws
- cardboard
- pencil
- black marker
- safety scissors
- glue

WHAT TO DO

1

Make sure your milk cartons are clean and dry, then glue the open ends so they are flattened and closed. One glued end will be the back of the small carton, and the other one will be the front of the large carton. Glue both backs together. Let dry.

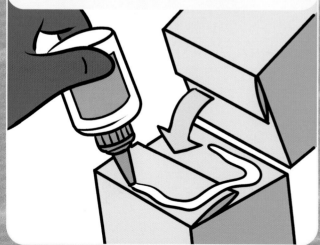

2

Paint the bottom half of the cartons gray—or silver if you have it!—and the top half of the cartons red. Let dry.

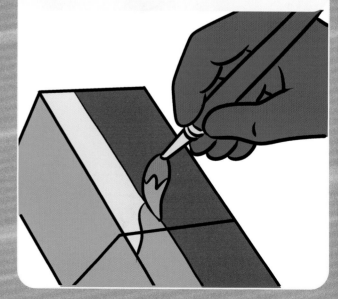

3 Carefully push a pencil through the cartons, twice on each side on each carton, where the wheels will be. Slot a straw through the front two holes in each carton, and another straw through the back two holes.

4 Ask an adult to help you cut out eight circles from cardboard, to be the wheels. Paint the cardboard circles black. Let dry. Carefully push a pencil through the center of each cardboard circle.

5 Slot a cardboard circle onto both ends of each straw. Trim the straw, leaving a little bit sticking out from the cardboard circles to stop them from falling off.

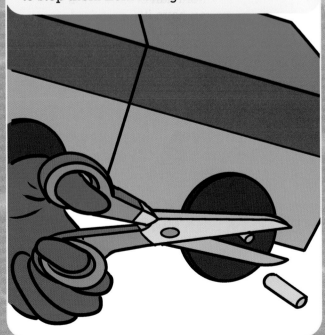

6 Carefully push a pencil twice through the end of each carton that used to be open, once on each side.

7 Push a pipe cleaner through the hole on the right side on the smaller carton, and then through the hole on the right side of the larger carton. Twist the pipe cleaner to create a closed loop, so the cartons are connected. Do the same with a pipe cleaner on the right side of the cartons.

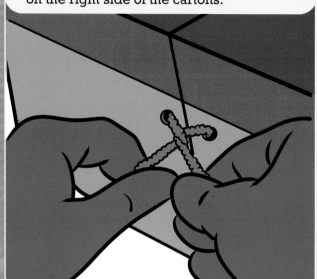

8 Pop out the PAW Patroller details from the back of the book and glue them onto the cartons. Let dry. Add any extra details with black marker.

ALL ABOARD THE PAW PATROLLER!

SUPER SLIDIN' SNOWBOARDS

Everest and Jake love to show the other pups how to speed down the mountain on their snowboards. It's SNOW much fun!

Make some mini snowboards by following these steps.

WHAT YOU NEED

- craft sticks
- pencil
- paintbrush
- paint

WHAT TO DO

Draw a pattern onto a craft stick using a pencil. Then paint the pattern. Let dry. Repeat with a different craft stick and pattern for each pup!

ICE OR SNOW,
WATCH THEM GO!